The SPICE Alphabet Book

herbs, spices, and other natural flavors

Spice up your life!

by Jerry Pallotta

illustrated by Leslie Evans

Leslie Evans

🏛 Charlesbridge

Copyright © 1994 by Jerry Pallotta.
Illustrations Copyright © 1994 by Leslie Evans.
Artist's Notes Copyright © 1994 by Leslie Evans.
All rights reserved, including the right of
reproduction in whole or in part in any form.

Published by
Charlesbridge Publishing
85 Main Street, Watertown, MA 02472
(617) 926-0329
www.charlesbridge.com

Printed in the United States of America
(sc) 10 9 8 7 6 5 4 3
(hc) 10 9 8 7 6 5 4 3

Printed on Recycled Paper

Library of Congress Cataloging-in-Publication Data
Pallotta, Jerry.
     The spice alphabet book: herbs, spices, and other
natural flavors / by Jerry Pallotta; illustrated by Leslie
Evans.
          p.   cm.
     ISBN 0-88106-898-5 (reinforced for library use)
     ISBN 0-88106-897-7 (softcover)
     1. Spices—Juvenile literature. 2. Herbs—
Juvenile literature. 3. English language—Alphabet—
Juvenile literature. [1. Spices. 2. Herbs. 3. Alphabet.]
I. Evans, Leslie. II. Title.
TX406.P27 1994
641.6'383 — dc20   94-5178
                                                CIP
                                                AC

Books by Jerry Pallotta:
  The Icky Bug Alphabet Book
  The Icky Bug Alphabet Board Book
  The Icky Bug Counting Book
  The Bird Alphabet Book
  The Ocean Alphabet Book
  The Flower Alphabet Book
  The Yucky Reptile Alphabet Book
  The Frog Alphabet Book
  The Furry Animal Alphabet Book
  The Dinosaur Alphabet Book
  The Underwater Alphabet Book
  The Victory Garden Vegetable Alphabet Book
  The Extinct Alphabet Book
  The Desert Alphabet Book
  The Butterfly Alphabet Book
  The Freshwater Alphabet Book
  The Airplane Alphabet Book
  The Boat Alphabet Book
  The Jet Alphabet Book
  Dory Story
  Going Lobstering
  Cuenta los insectos (The Icky Bug Counting Book)
  The Crayon Counting Book
  The Crayon Counting Board Book
  Underwater Counting: Even Numbers

*Coca-Cola, Coke, the contour bottle and the Dynamic
Ribbon device are trademarks of The Coca-Cola
Company.*

*The Lavender Water is used with permission from
Crabtree & Evelyn.*

*HERSHEY'S, HERSHEY'S HUGS, HERSHEY'S
KISSES, and the Conical Configuration and attached
Plume Device are registered trademarks and used with
permission.*

*Thank you BAKER'S® Chocolate Company. Reprinted
with the permission of Kraft General Foods, Inc.*

Thank you to author Theodore Taylor for Yaupon.

A zillion thanks to
Dr. Arthur "Sonny" Pallotta,
biochemist, toxicologist, scientist,
uncle, and above all, friend.

These illustrations are dedicated in memory
of my wonderful mother, Shirley Mays Evans.

Many thanks to Pamela Ryan and Rosalie Davis
for their help in the preparation of this book.

Aa

A is for Anise. Anise is a spice that comes from a seed and tastes like licorice. *What is a spice?*

A spice is the section of a plant that has the flavor. The spice flavor could be from the bark, the stem, the flower, the bean, the nut, the oil, the sap, the seed, the leaf, or the root of a plant.

Anise seeds
.75 ¼ lb

THAYERS
HONEY &
ANISE
COUGH
SYRUP
WITH BEE PROPOLIS
4 FL. OZ.

anise drops

jelly beans

ANIS PASTILLES
NET WT 1¾ OZ.

anise oil
½ FL. OZ.

GINGER
99¢ POUND

FRESH
CILANTRO
2 FOR 1 50

basil

FRESH BASIL
1 50 EXTRA FANCY
BUNCH

DILL
2 FOR 1 50

FARMER'S BEST

Bb

GARLIC
99¢ POUND

WATERCRESS
2 FOR 1 50

TOMATOES
79¢ POUND

B is for Basil. Basil is an herb. If you go to market, walk near the fresh Basil and take a good whiff. It smells wonderful. *What is an herb?*

An herb is an edible green leaf that is used to season foods.

Cc

C is for Cinnamon. Cinnamon comes from the bark of a tree. At one time, Cinnamon was more valuable than gold. The demand for spices, such as Cinnamon, encouraged explorers to search for a shorter route to India.

INDIA

SRI LANKA

Cinnamon
.50 OZ

Dd

D is for Dill. Whenever you say the word Dill, people immediately think of pickles. Dill peanut butter, Dill ice cream, and Dill milk do not sound right. Dill pickles sounds perfect!

dill weed
.90 oz.

Ee

E is for Eucalyptus. When you had a cold, maybe someone rubbed your chest with Eucalyptus salve or gave you a Eucalyptus cough drop. Or, maybe you took a bath that steamed up the room with the smell of Eucalyptus.

F is for Fennel. Fennel is an herb and a spice. All parts of the plant are edible. You can eat the fresh or dried green leaves. You can use the seeds for baking. You can also eat the stalk and bulb like a piece of celery.

Ff

Gg

G is for Garlic. Garlic has a powerful flavor! If you eat a lot of Garlic on Monday, someone might still smell it on your breath on Tuesday or even Wednesday. But, don't worry. Eating Garlic is good for you.

WELCOME TO GILROY GARLIC CAPITAL OF THE WORLD

G is also for Ginger. The Ginger flavor comes from a root. It has a taste that is hard to describe. If you bite into raw Ginger, it seems to bite back.

Have you ever made a gingerbread house?

Molasses Spice Crisps
Grandma
2½ cups sifted flour
2 tsp each of ginger, cloves, cinnamon and baking soda—
Sift flour once, measure and add soda + spices
Sift together 3 times
Cream ¾ cup shortening, add 1 cup sugar gradually and cream together
Add 1 egg unbeaten-beat well. Then add 4 Tbsp molasses, flour and mix thoroughly
Chill dough – roll in balls and dip in sugar
Place on greased cookie sheet
Bake 15 to 20 minutes at 350°

Vernors
deliciously different!

Ginger
.50-oz

Thou shalt not steal

Hh

H is for Herb Garden. If you want to grow an Herb Garden, you do not need much room. You can grow one in a window box, between the rungs of a ladder, or even in an old boat. Your Herb Garden might attract a hummingbird and a few butterflies.

HYSSOP

herb

Shirley Seeds

Habanero
PEPPER

HOT STUFF
MUÑOZ SEEDS

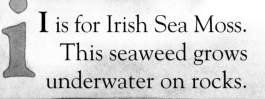

I is for Irish Sea Moss. This seaweed grows underwater on rocks.

It is harvested, dried, and made into a powder called carrageen. In foods, it keeps ingredients mixed together, otherwise the flavorings would sink to the bottom or float to the top.

It's time for a COFFEE BREAK!

J is for Java. Java is another name for coffee. Java is also an island in Indonesia where coffee is grown. Think of all the vocabulary that includes the word coffee, such as coffee table, coffee cake, coffee pot, and coffee break!

OCIA certified
ORGAN...
Pluma
Coixtepec
STRICTLY HIGH GROWN
OAXACA
Mexico

CAFÉ DO BRASIL
/23 02/0
KENYA A
LOT G
BREM...

Y S
YAUCO SELECTO
HIGH MOUNTAIN GROWN
SHIPPED BY: YAUCO SELECTO, S.E.
NET WEIGHT 100 LBS.(45.36KG.)
PREMIUM COFFEE GROWN IN PUERTO-RICO,
SIZE: A
★ GRACIAS A LOS CORSOS

SAN FRANCISCO
COFFEE BEANS
PRODUCE OF JAVA
INDONESIA
1-200

MATARI
O. YEMEN

Coca-Cola

Kk

K is for Kola.
Kola nuts are the seeds from the Kola tree
that grows in tropical Africa. One of the most
popular drinks in the world is a soda flavored
with an extract made from Kola nuts.

L is for Lavender. If we were going to eat or drink all of the great tasting things in this book, it would be a good idea to wash our hands first. Lavender is a fragrance used in making soap.

CAN THESE GUYS CUT THE MUSTARD?

CITGO

Dijon •

FRANCE

Please SOX R H E INN pass
CUBS 1

SOX 1 2 3 4 5 6 7 8 9 10 R H E
CUBS

Crab

Mustard Seed

Mm

M is for Mustard. People often associate tastes and smells with places they have been. The smell of Mustard can bring back the memory of a home run, with the bases loaded, in the bottom of the ninth inning. This spice can take you out to the ball game!

Mm

M is also for Maple. This flavor comes from the sap of certain Maple trees. When it is tapped, the sap is very watery. After it is boiled, it thickens and becomes delicious Maple syrup.

JACK & JILL

Maple Candy

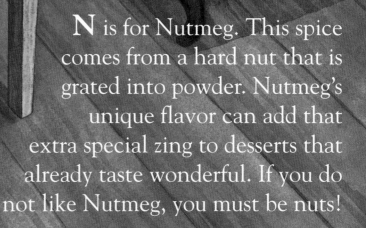

N is for Nutmeg. This spice comes from a hard nut that is grated into powder. Nutmeg's unique flavor can add that extra special zing to desserts that already taste wonderful. If you do not like Nutmeg, you must be nuts!

whole
nutmeg

mace

Oo

O is for Oregano. Oregano is often used to flavor tomato sauce. Tomato sauce is used on top of spaghetti and pizza. The person who wrote this book loves pizza. Do you?

oros ganos

oregano
.50 oz

Pp

P is for Pepper. Just thinking about this page . . . Ah ah ah . . . can make you ah ah ah ah . . . Sneeze! AH CHOO! It wouldn't be fair to mention pepper without mentioning salt.

Salt is a flavor, but it does not come from a plant. Salt is a mineral.

SUPER HOT CHILI

cayenne .50-oz

pepper-corns

Qq

Q is for Quinine. Quinine comes from the bark of a cinchona tree. It gives a bitter flavoring to the carbonated drink called tonic water. It is also a medicine. During the construction of the Panama Canal, many workers got sick from malaria and were treated with Quinine.

parsley   sage   rosemary   thyme

Rr

R is for Rosemary.
This herb feels and smells
like pine needles. Rosemary
has always been known as
the herb of remembrance.
It is nice to send a sprig of
Rosemary to a person you love.

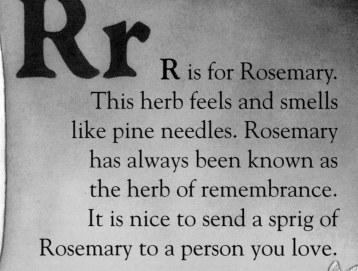

rosemary leaves

Ss

S is for Spearmint.

Spearmint and peppermint are aromatic herbs that are used to flavor candy, gum, and toothpaste. It is fun to eat candy, but don't forget to brush your teeth.

T should be for tea, but it's not.

T is for Tarragon. Tarragon is an herb that is popular in gourmet kitchens. Great chefs around the world have been cooking with it for hundreds of years.

Uu

U is for Uva-ursi.
Uva-ursi is also called bearberry.
People do not usually eat Uva-ursi.
Bears love to eat it, but bears
cannot read this book.

V v

V is for Vanilla. Vanilla is the most popular ice cream flavor in the world. The Vanilla bean comes from the pod of an orchid flower. This flavor was discovered in the tropical rain forest.

PURE
Vanilla
extract

ICE CREAM

ICE CREAM

SOLD It's
Pure
Cream HERE

BUY
THEM
HERE

GOOD HUMOR ICE CREAM CO.

"Good Humors"

2

Thank you, rain forest.

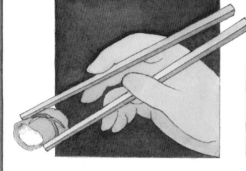

Ww

W is for Wasabi. The bright green stuff on your plate at a sushi restaurant is a hot spice that comes from the root of the Wasabi plant. If you try Wasabi, only take a teeny-weeny taste.

When the people of Central and South America discovered it, they thought it was a gift from the gods. Today, people worldwide still consider it to be the ultimate flavor.

X is for Xocoatl. Xocoatl is the Aztec word for chocolate.

Yy

Here is the tea page!

Y is for Yaupon. Many years ago, when
people could not afford to buy tea,
they brewed their own from the leaves
of the Yaupon holly bush. Today,
herbal teas are
still very popular.